Medicine, Music
and Mirth

Compiled and edited by

Jennifer D. Maree

Other books by this author:
Ubuntu, the spirit of African Transformation
Blending cultures: a moving story

Inquiries should be made to:
Seaview Press
PO Box 7339
West Lakes, South Australia 5021
Telephone 08 8242 0666; fax 08 8242 0333
E-mail: seaview@seaviewpress.com.au
Web site: http://www.seaviewpress.com.au

Printed by:
Salmat Document Management Solutions Pty Limited
11 James Congdon Drive, Mile End, South Australia 5031.

National Library of Australia Cataloguing-in-Publication entry
Author: Maree, Jennifer D.
Title: Medicine, music and mirth / author, Jennifer D. Maree.
Publisher: West Lakes, S. Aust. : Seaview Press, 2007.
ISBN: 9781740084840 (pbk.)
Subjects: Allnut, Isabella Thirza Wright, 1930-
             Nurses--South Africa--Biography.

Dewey Number: 610.73092

To my wonderful mother,

Is Allnutt (nee Lombard)

born 13th of September 1930,
who gave up so much for us,
while showing enormous strength and stamina
and keeping life extremely interesting.

To other members of my family
who died before making old bones;
my brothers, Jonathan and Andrew, my uncle John
and my cousins, Lynne, Edith, Timothy and Pat.

Acknowledgements

To all those who so freely contributed to this book. I requested stories and tributes from all my mother's friends and family, that I had addresses for, and I want to thank Gaynor, Beth, Margaret (2), Mavis, Virginia, Donna, Erica, Brenda, Eva, Dot, Edith, Jean, Carole, Joan, Ena, Marion, Prinea, Gwen and Leon for responding. This book is not intended to be sold for profit, it is a memoir of a very special character for family and friends, but should profit be made, it will go to the Adrenoleukodystrophy Foundation.

I would also like to thank Margaret Horn, Carol Tudor Jones and Leon Maree for assistance with the book.

The Author

Jenny Maree has consulted to organizations, teams and individuals on effective management practices for over twenty years. She has trained and consulted in many countries, holding positions such as Asia Pacific Learning and Development Manager for ACE Insurance, based in Sydney and Academic Director, De Montfort University, based in Johannesburg. She has spoken at conferences on change management, mentoring and performance management, lectured at under and post graduate level on Organisational Behaviour and written books and articles on leadership, cultural change and outsourcing.

Contents

"It is of immense importance to learn to laugh at ourselves."

Katherine Mansfield

"This above all – to thine own self be true,
And it must follow, as night follows day,
Thou canst not then be false to any man."

William Shakespeare

Introduction

Mom was a very special person, not easy to forget and if she liked you, fantastic company — but if she did not, not such a pleasure. She had an interesting relationship with the truth, she could not lie and anything that made her feel that she was in any way doing so, made her extremely uncomfortable. Even a white lie was difficult, so this meant that social niceties were often forgotten, but her words were often so outrageous that she produced much laughter. This book has been compiled to capture some of her essence and, in the process, remember the joy that she brought so many. Sometimes by saying what everybody couldn't, sometimes by helping someone through nursing them, sometimes by providing a role model to other women experiencing difficulties.

My mother had four possible solutions for every kind of problem. If you were over 18, it involved medicine, music, sex or humour and if you were under 18, it involved all those except sex.

If she met someone and they were grumpy or less than agreeable, they were not getting enough sex. If she then decided that they were actually getting enough sex, than she would try music as an alternative solution, and if that was not successful, then medicine. If all else failed, my mother would resort to her permanent fallback position for everything in life — humour.

People loved to be with her, because she was a tonic. Much of the time, people were unaware of her enormous other talents because she spent so much time making them laugh that they did not get to see how organised she was, how she got things done, how punctual she was, how reliable she was and how well she nursed and played the piano. If she promised you something at a certain time in a certain condition, you would get it just as she promised. She hated to owe money, always wanted to pay her way and always did. Whatever she achieved, be it getting her matric/university qualifications (at a mature age) or nursing qualifications, acquiring possessions or purchasing her property, she did it on her own.

I will always remember her as honest, straightforward, strong, patriotic, proud, compassionate, sensitive, stubborn, vulnerable, caring, giving, loyal, listening, opinionated, feminine, popular, resilient, gregarious, funny, wild and wise. She wanted us both to be lawyers so that we could fight for women's rights. My sister listened to her and became a lawyer.

She had some favourite sayings, such as, "What you sow so shall you reap" and then her advice on men, which again she would give to anyone willing to hear it:

"Men are only interested in their stomachs and what hangs from them!"

"A man will treat you the way he treats his car!"

"Don't marry a Hollander, they are too fastidious!"

"Don't go out with cricketers, they won't treat you well!"

"Marry a man who can fix things!"

She also had some favourite poets, authors and artists. She had a painting by Theunis De Jong that she loved, she had Rudyard Kipling's poem "If" up on the wall and always her copper mermaid — she took up the art of copper at some stage. She loved the story of the little mermaid by Hans Christian Andersen. Perhaps she would have loved to be the little mermaid and be near the sea permanently.

This is my record of some of the stories my mother told us about her life and what I remember about her and those stories.

You may remember others or have different recollections of these events. If so, I would love to hear from you through my website on www.jennymareeconsulting.com. I would love to hear from any of my mother's family or friends and will reply to all letters.

Earliest memory

The earliest memory I have of my mother is going to the beach for Christmas day and having the loveliest picnic of ham, Kitka bread (she bought this every Saturday) and pickles with my dad, sister and brothers. It must have been before disaster struck our little family and Jonathan and Andrew became terminally ill. There were no more beach Christmases after that.

My mother loved the sea and always wanted to call a home "La Mare" but this never happened. Perhaps this love developed because she grew up inland in Johannesburg. At least she had a daughter who gained a last name close to that name!

1.

Is' early years
– before marriage

To understand my mother, one needs to meet my grandparents. Thirza Guscott married John Lombard (Lommie). Lommie and Thirza had met in a boarding house in Hillbrow. He was much older than Thirza and had left his sweetheart behind in the Cape. He had arrived from Tulbagh, with a characteristic Western Cape bray, in the big city of gold, Johannesburg, to make his fortune. He met Thirza who had china blue eyes and was a little over five feet and promptly forgot all about Emmie in the Cape. For the rest of his life he always took his holiday in the Cape alone and Emmie, a music teacher, never married. It was assumed by the family, but never discussed, that he spent some time with Emmie every year in the Cape.

Mom was born in 1930 and this was not easy information to get as age was something that my mom and grandmother did not like to reveal. She always took great pride in her appearance and I never saw her outside her bedroom without make-up on.

She was a beautiful baby, the youngest of three children. The elder brother John, died of diphtheria. This was a fatal disease in those days. His death was a very traumatic event in the family and, according to a family member, one which made her brother Roland, called Roy, become an even more precious and favoured child. Is grew up in Orange Grove in Johannesburg and was always embarrassed about the area. I went back to live there when I moved to Johannesburg and she really hated me going back to her roots, but when I got there, it was a good area. She attended a convent school there and wanted to be a nun. At one stage, the family lived in a house — I recall this because my mom used to tell the story of my grandfather, who I never met, coming into her bedroom one night and seeing some feet going through the window. Her father chased the man down the street with my mom's hockey stick. I don't think he caught him, but they never had any trouble after that as my grandfather became very notorious in the neighbourhood for his temper, not to mention that he was over six feet tall.

They never had much money, so I don't think they ever owned a property or a car. Their next move was to a flat in Orange Grove which was a delight for Mom as the apartment block was owned by a childless couple called Beatrice and Emmanuel Papendakis. They were to become lifelong friends of my mother and family. Auntie Bea, who I got to know very well too, was very kind to Mom. The tea room on the corner was also owned by Uncle Emmanuel and the neighbourhood all loved to purchase their necessities there. Auntie Bea was known for her charm and white gloves. Uncle Emmanuel was a very wise and astute businessman, while Auntie Bea came from a large Seventh Day Adventist family (Davies) and they were all also very kind to all of us. Every Christmas, Uncle Emmanuel would carry boxes and boxes of biscuits to all his suppliers. Every teller in the Orange Grove Standard Bank received a huge box of biscuits and there were many other companies that did too. Every Greek Easter we would have lovely red boiled eggs on the table and the tastiest rice pudding and syrupy cake and everyone would say "Christus Arnesti!" and "Gronje Pola" to all the visitors at their lovely homely flat. When Auntie Bea and Uncle Emmanuel died, my mother said it was like a close member of her family dying.

My maternal grandfather, Lommy, worked for the Standard Bank as a teller and the story goes that if anyone gave him cheek, he had no problem climbing over the counter and letting them feel his unhappiness. According to my mom, he was never promoted, because he had the wrong last name, Lombard, and also because of his temper.

The flat in Orange Grove only had one bedroom so Mom slept on a divan in the lounge. Roy volunteered for military service when World War II broke out and was sent up north. My mom always said this was his way of escaping the unhappy household.

Mom left school at 16 as money was short — my grandfather was well known for his love of the horses (he died at the racecourse!) and my gran, Thirza, struggled to make ends meet. She took in sewing, knitted, crocheted, baked and was famous for making a meal out of nothing. She would buy fish each Friday and pickle, fry or grill it.

My mother tried secretarial work and did not enjoy it. Her first boss was horrible and she hated the routine of the office. Thirza made her first work outfit out of old curtains. Isobel found it very hard living at home with her parents, as they were continuously bickering. Lommie would walk around singing "My Sarie Marais" and Thirza would walk around singing "There Will Always Be an England". Poor Lommy could not get comfortable anywhere, as Thirza would be fluffing the cushions and working her feather duster overtime.

Mom decided to leave home and went to nurses' college in Boksburg, where she met Daphne. When Roy came home from the war, Mom took her nursing friend Daphne to meet the train and they eventually married. They had three children: Lynne, Graham and Trevor. Both Roy and Daph worked very hard in their businesses, initially a garage in Northcliff, Johannesburg. Roy worked as a mechanic and through his hard work and entrepreneurship he progressively acquired a number of service stations. Uncle Wilfred Guscott, brother of Thirza, then summoned him to Port Elizabeth (PE) and wanted him to buy into the family hotel. Roy decided to settle in PE and when Uncle Wilfred emigrated to Australia, Roy bought the Beach hotel from him. Roy and Daphne lived in a beautiful double-storey house on Brighton Drive and then in a luxurious flat in Bandle, both in Summerstrand. For us as children, it was a lifestyle we could only imagine. We saw them now and then, but it was our only exposure to the world of yachts, sports-cars, mansions, millionaires, boats, holiday houses and finishing schools.

Somewhere along the line, Mom learned to play the piano. Writing a book about your mother gives you a chance to reflect on so much and, as I write this, I am wondering if perhaps Grandpa influenced my mom's love of music through the great love of his life, Emmie the music teacher in the Boland of the Cape or, as suggested by another family member, if it was inherited from great-granny Minnie Guscott, also a music teacher. My mother adored and respected her father and never said a bad word about him. She always said that she would have so loved for him to have seen her first child. My other thought is that perhaps my mother loved her cars so much because she adored her older brother, Roy, who also had a love for cars.

She was an enormously talented pianist and all through her life was begged to play the piano. She knew and loved the classics, collected all sorts of mementos of the great composers and any musical instrument. She played jazz, syncopation, classics and any music that took her fancy. She had an ability I always wished I had, which is to play music by ear. When I was little and decisions were to be made about extracurricular activities during the school years, my mother would not hear of us doing ballet, as she said that we could play the piano until we died, but dancing had limited years and application. I studied the piano for many years. It warmed my mother's heart. Her piano was always her second most prized possession, next to her car. It was so devastating when she had to sell these two possessions to move to Park Drive Retirement Village years later. One of her favourite sayings was, "always be welcome in people's homes, be useful". She felt that people always welcomed her because she could entertain them through the piano and nurse them if they were sick. The irony was that people loved having my mother around anyway, she was so amusing.

My mom's political views were quite a feature of her life and there are many stories of various incidents where she would be very vocal in her opinions, no matter who was there to hear them. One time, a politician phoned her to get her vote and by the time she had finished her stories and he could get off the phone, he had been convinced in another direction. He never phoned again. I would also have loved to have been a fly on the wall when she was one of the key members of the body corporate meetings in her townhouse complex.

Whatever my mother's political views, she said many things to shock people and get a laugh, but deep down she spent her life nursing mostly the poorest people of South Africa. During her initial nursing years, she nursed in partnership with Nelson Mandela's first wife, Evelyn, in Orlando Township. They became good friends and my mom assisted her with her divorce. They used to drive out into the location (in apartheid times, these were designated black areas), open up the boot of the car, which was loaded with sweeties, and wait for the children to come running out of the shacks so that they could give them injections against diseases like Tuberculosis (TB). She had many, many nursing friends and all are unanimous about her dedication to anyone and everyone she nursed. We used to love to be sick because my mom would treat us like royalty. The bedroom was immediately turned in to a ward and the usual 24-hour care was even more targeted. I remember the little tray she would set with all the medicines lined up. The beds were made and remade to the neatness standards of the military.

For many of our school years, she worked at Empilweni Hospital, where she nursed TB patients. Many of these patients spent years and years in this hospital, without visitors. My mother treated them with deep care and respect and was loved by both staff and patients. Only later in life, did she realise her dream of becoming a matron, when she left public hospitals. I am sure that you can picture my mom surrounded by bureaucrats, rather hard to imagine! You would not expect to find someone like my mom in a government department. She has often been described as a "free spirit". She was too much of a free spirit to be considered for promotion in the government and she had very clear opinions of the favouritism that existed there.

Again, one reflects on a life, and my mother was very deeply affected by an incident in her youth in Orange Grove. It gave her tremendous compassion, but also much guilt. She used to love to visit the roof of their block of flats on Louis Botha Ave, Orange Grove. It was a good place to get away from the constant bickering of Thirza and Lommy. One day, she was looking over the balcony and saw a black man get kicked to death. He had done nothing, except walk past the Radium Beer Hall and, bad luck for him, three drunken men happened to come out at that moment and that was the end of him. My mother was so traumatised that she stood frozen on the roof. She spent her life thinking about what she should have done. There would have been no easy answer in apartheid South Africa with a mother raised in England (she was sent there during the war years to be brought up by her aunt and trained as a milliner) and a father from the Boland.

The matron of the Park Village Retirement Centre remembers my mother well as a great teacher and mentor of other nurses. She tells many good stories of how my mother taught them to swear as well as nurse!

2.

Mom's first marriage

Mom was married three times by the age of 29 and told us very little about the first two husbands.

The first one's name was Peter. I do know his last name, but in any event would prefer not to use it as I don't know his current circumstances.

Peter was apparently a real casanova and, according to my mother, she came home one day after six months of marriage and found him in bed with her best friend. She divorced him on the spot.

These are stories my mother told many times, but I never thought to ask any questions about this man. What job did he have? How old was he? How did she meet him? Where was he born? I know none of that. I think he may have come from the East Rand of Johannesburg and played in a band.

I remember when I was very young, my mother calling me to the kitchen in our house in Humewood in PE and taking a match to a photo in the newspaper. I think it was "People on the Move" in the *Sunday Times* and I think there was a photo of Peter there, and my mother said she wanted me to know that he was gone out of her life. I am not sure why she needed to tell me that, as I was a child of her third husband and he was her first, so I would not have given that sort of thing a thought. Maybe it helped her gain some closure.

3.

Mom's second marriage

M y mom told the story of how, in the 1950s, if you were a divorced woman, people treated you with such suspicion and she really struggled for friends and the men would treat her like she was "easy". If you know my mother, you will know that that was one thing she never was, in more ways than one. When she met Jack, she was so touched by the fact that he made no such advances. He treated her like a queen, took her to wonderful jazz venues, was highly cultured and sophisticated and worked as an advocate. The only drawback was that he was the only child born to a gynaecologist father and a very possessive mother. This was, however, not the cause of the divorce. The problem in the end was that in two years of marriage, Jack never did make any of those advances. The saddest part is that he moved back in with his mother, and after a few years, drank himself to death after they were divorced. You will note that some of the other tributes I have received describe this differently.

4.

My mom's third marriage and the deaths of Jonathan and Andrew

I am the eldest child born to this marriage. My mother was 29 when she met George, who was 23. I was born early in the marriage before my father had qualified as a Chartered Accountant, so money was tight. My mother had worked very hard to save money and was able to assist with buying their first house.

Mom went on to have three more children – Jonathan, Angela and Andrew. Jonathan died in 1972 and Andrew in 1973 after a long terminal illness. It was heart-rendering to watch children being taken bit by bit. One by one, each of the senses shut down.

Mom loved to watch cricket and also play it. She always had a favourite sportsman in each sport. We had wonderful next-door neighbours in Ferndale Rd, Humewood, Mr and Mrs Eddy. When their very good-looking grandsons used to visit, mom used to play cricket with them on the Eddy's lawn. She used to play cricket with many of the young men in the family or children of her friends. She was a real sport. She said that in her youth she had wished she could be a boy. She loved all their sports and in those days girls could not play them at school. You would not like to have met my mother on a hockey field or anywhere when she was carrying her hockey stick. She once told a story about a man who followed her home one day after a hockey match. If he did not feel her hockey stick, you can be sure that he got threatened with it. All I know is that whatever had been bought at the shop was spilt all over the lift.

Mom spent several years nursing Jonathan and Andrew. They slowly went from attending schools and playing, like other children, to bed-ridden vegetables. Their initial years were pretty normal and so my mom only noticed the disease when they started showing signs of not hearing or seeing as well as could be expected. Jonathan was constantly tripping. Mom was enormously good at detecting signs of illness and helped several people over the years diagnose problems with their children or family members. She had an innate gut instinct for diagnosis and would often surprise doctors with her quick assessment of a medical situation. She was a born nurse. It makes you think how long it might have taken some other parent to pick up what Jonathan and Andrew had. Even with all her medical knowledge and experience she traipsed from doctor to doctor and was sent in all directions to get a diagnosis. Finally she saw a brain surgeon, Dr Kessler, and he assisted her to get the help that she needed and this seemed to necessitate several visits to Johannesburg. In Johannesburg, a Dr Mechanic was very helpful with Jonathan and had deep respect for the way my mother handled the situation and also helped mom determine whether Angela and I were going to get this mystery disease too. ALD (Adrenoleukodystrophy) in those days was fairly rare. It was before the movie *Lorenzo's Oil* (starring Nick Nolte and Susan

Sarandon and directed by George Miller, an Australian) had put the disease on the map. We were the first family in South Africa to be affected with this disease that we knew of. My mom helped several affected families thereafter. My mom offered both my brothers' bodies for research, but there was little interest in such a rare disease. She did communicate with some academics for many years to try and keep abreast. Dr Hugo Moser was a significant support to my mother throughout my brothers' illness. On many occasions there was no one else who had the knowledge or who was as accessible as he was, although based in America.

ALD is caused by a genetic mutation that leads to the accumulation of substances called very long chain fatty acids in cells. That, in turn, damages the myelin, the material that coats nerve fibers in the brain, much like the insulating material that protects telephone wire. The myelin damage is irreversible and is what causes the neurological system to break down. (Extract from International Herald Tribune Americas, Jan 23, 2007 Dr Hugo Moser dies, work was depicted in "Lorenzo's oil".)

Ange is working as a lawyer now and still lives in PE while I run my own management consulting business in Australia. I specialize in change management, spending a large proportion of time helping organizations, teams and individuals to deal with loss in many shapes and forms.

5.

The divorce

Jonathan died aged eleven and to add to this distress, the marriage floundered. There was a lot of conflict about the origins of my brothers' illness. My parents were divorced in 1972 and my dad remarried soon after. Between marriages he lived in number 6 Selwyn Court in Summerstrand in a huge three-bed-roomed flat. We used to love to visit him there and take our beautiful dog, Teddy. Teddy was Jonathan's dog, so very dear to us. He jumped off my father's balcony one day and landed on the ground – this was a three-story fall and somehow he was fine. He later disappeared and this broke our hearts.

My father's new wife had two children and he moved into their American-Colonial style house in Summerstrand. Her husband had been killed in the 1972 Heathrow air crash. She showed me his watch once, full of bloodstains and pretty horrific, which the airline had sent her long after the crash. Shirley came from a large farming family from the Cathcart area in the Eastern Cape. She had three brothers, Raymond, Aubrey and Michael. They were hugely impactful in her life and therefore in ours. Raymond was married to Mary and had four children, Stephen, Angela, Mark and Carol, and they lived on the farm Ravenshaw. Aubrey was married to Lorraine and had three children, Debbie, Sandra and Ailsa. Ailsa was also the name of their farm. Michael was married to a beautiful Dutch lady, Marguerite, and their children were Michael, Peter, Grace and Francis. He and Aubrey were farming neighbours as well as brothers. We had many wonderful farming holidays on their farms and I learned to serve in the shop and speak quite a bit of Xhosa through this. We also rode horses and I learned to love another part of nature. My mom had taught me to love the sea and now I learned to love the bush. We spent many lovely hours at my father's house in Summerstrand, swimming in their pool on our alternate weekends with them.

My father seldom visited the dying Andrew once he was remarried. He, Shirley and their families took very little interest in the nursing and subsequent death of Andrew. This is not meant as a judgement. I realise now how many people do not know what to do and those that supported us were mostly religious or medical. In these two professions, people are especially trained in the handling of grief and loss. My mom, sister and I shared one bedroom, while Andrew lay dying in the other.

My mom was very alone at the funerals, except for the wonderful support of Daphne, Lynne, Ossie (Lynne's boyfriend, a pharmacist) and her wonderful friends, as always.

We lived in a townhouse in Cathcart Gardens and my mom ended up living in that complex for at least 30 years.

6.

The Lombards

Lynne's death

I have mentioned my brothers' deaths which were very traumatic for my mother, but she kept herself going by nursing them herself. Only near the end, when they required regular turning to avoid bedsores, did she get in help. When they could no longer be fed, she had to send them to hospital so they could feed intravenously. She also kept herself going by getting a society going for other ALD families and keeping in regular contact with Professor Moser, an expert on ALD who lived in the USA.

When her niece, Lynne, died of an asthma attack in her early 30's, it had a devastating effect on my mother. Auntie Daphne, Lynne and her boyfriend, Ozzic, had been so fantastic during my brothers' illnesses that I think she could not believe that such ill fortune could come to them. Ossie carried one of my brothers to hospital.

After the funeral we went to Vaughan and Janella Brittle's house, where my mom got the drunkest I have ever seen her — I could not get her to stay in the car, to drive her home. On the way home, I think a leg or arm was sticking out the window, but Ange helped me to hold her in. She told me some things that I have never repeated and I have never let her know that she told me, because I think she would deny them. The Brittle family has also been a wonderful support to our family over the years. Vaughan's mother and my grandmother were best friends. Vaughan was best friends with my cousin, Graeme, who achieved success in the army, becoming a senior officer. Vaughan previously dated one of my best friend's sisters and my mom has always been so fond of Vaughan and all his family.

My mother loved all her brother's children so much and felt their losses almost as much as if they were her own children. She was always very close to Lynn and Graeme and, in her later years, Trevor. Trevor added to the hotel empire, taking it to greater heights of achievement.

Lynne's funeral was very traumatic for me, as she had befriended my stepmother — how was I going to handle this social occasion? My mother would not speak to me if I even acknowledged my stepmother at the funeral or anywhere else. My mom had all her spies (her friends), who would report to her if I even so much as smiled at my stepmother. The consequences were too awful to contemplate.

Roy's death

Uncle Roy had been such a key person in our lives. Although we had seen so little of him, he had featured so prominently in my mother's stories about her childhood and her relationship with her mother.

The Lombard's lived such a different life to us that we did not really cross paths. I recall the local minister bumping in to my mom at Pick and Pay supermarket and commenting "What are you doing shopping here, your brother is Roy Lombard!"

When Roy died of cancer, we did not hesitate to get on a plane and fly down from Johannesburg, where we were working, for his funeral. My mother phoned to try and stop me, saying, "why are you coming, he has left you nothing in his will." That did not even occur to me as he was a significant player in her life and that alone meant that we would go to the funeral.

She was so proud of Roy and his achievements and was always ready to tell people how Roy had done it all on his own. She never took any handouts from him and was proud of that. Once she loaned him a blue Italian Spode plate for the opening of the Bell Restaurant at the Beach Hotel. She never stopped reminding him, and until the last time we went to that restaurant for dinner, she reminded me to make sure that I got that plate back from Trevor as it belonged to her!

Daphne's death

If you want to understand my mother, you need to know how much Roy and Daphne meant to her. They were really her anchor. When she had been divorced twice and was sick of nursing, she went to Port Elizabeth to work for Roy and Daphne at the Beach Hotel. She worked as a receptionist and there she met my dad, who was working as an accountant. She saw each child grow up and Auntie Dot, Auntie Daphne's mother, was very dear to her. In the end Auntie Dot and my gran, Thirza, lived in the same block of flats, Grosvenor Court, with Yvonne Brittle in the block of flats in front. My gran used to tend the marigold garden at the flats, which she loved. She was so industrious and had such a routine. Every day she baked, cooked or sewed. She used to crochet bags out of supermarket packets, make her own lemon cool drink and bake short-bread. I used to love to visit her, but my mother dreaded it. She always felt that her mother preferred Roy in every way. We all had to be carefully inspected before visiting my gran as, according to my mother, she was very critical and we had to be on our best behaviour. We had to dress specially, polish our shoes, brush our hair and sit very straight while visiting granny. We would have our necks scrubbed, always a very painful experience, before each visit.

When Daphne died, my mother felt like her own mother had died again. When her own mother died, she said that it was like someone had taken away her roots, but now it seemed to her like the last person connected to her childhood had gone.

Daphne had visited Mom, the night she died, in a terrible state. She had begged my mother to help her children leave South Africa. She had always done work at various charities and had spent time with one of the many orphans that she befriended and they had been very rude to her and grabbed her cross from around her neck very violently and threatened her. She had taken in orphans and looked after them in various ways all her life. She was also a devout Christian and considered herself reborn. She was very clearly rattled, as she was usually a very calm and serene person. Mom was very worried about her. She also would not normally arrive unannounced at my mom's flat. That night she died of a heart attack. My mother had terrible guilt about it, as they had phoned her from the hospital and told her to come, but she was too scared to drive at night. Mom had supported Daphne through her divorce from Roy and this had created a close bond. I am not sure if Roy ever understood how his sister could support his ex-wife in preference to him, but my mother always took the women's part, especially if infidelity was involved.

I heard about her death too late to come to South Africa from Australia for the funeral. I regret that.

7.

Eccentricities

My mother had many eccentric habits, which her friends delighted in, but as her daughter, I used to get very embarrassed. She had a wicked sense of humour and would think nothing of taking a huge cockroach to a restaurant and causing a stir by placing it in the middle of a dish and then complaining to the manager of the restaurant about the food. This produced great hilarity.

She was also known for getting a whole restaurant dancing on the tables.

Craft

We received a letter from my mom with these letters in it. I phoned her to see what they meant and she said that if someone asked her how she was feeling, she would say, "I am fine, except for a bit of CRAFT." I asked her what that meant and she said "Can't remember a f........ thing!" This was when she was getting dementia. She actually told me that she thought she was getting Alzheimer's. I asked her how this related to Jonathan and Andrew, but that subject was always a closed topic. It is interesting to read about carriers on the ALD website.

AMTC

We received several postcards from my mom on one of her trips somewhere exotic with just these letters on the back and a picture of a pretty building on front. I telephoned her on her return to get clarification. She said, "Another f.... church!" She said these tours just consisted of visits to churches. She would far rather have visited all the old pubs!

Boyfriends

I took a boyfriend to her flat in Cathcart Gardens. She told me that I had to take my sister out on the date, too. I gave in. That was the last time he asked me out.

She would not serve dinner to another because she did not like the way he spoke. I had to talk my way out of that one. He also never dated me again.

Frugality

Mom was very frugal and managed to save very well. Much of the time we ate leftovers from the hospital. My mom grew up in the war years and could not bear to throw food or pantyhose away. What the patients did not eat at the hospital and was going to go in the rubbish bin, she brought home instead. This helped us in many ways, but she never lowered her standards regarding buying clothes, shoes, food and cosmetics. She would only shop at Garlicks, where she felt you got proper service. She thought it very below standard to shop at Woolworths! Shoes had to be leather and bras had to be properly fitted by someone who was trained. Meat was bought from a butcher. In later years, she started to buy meat at Pick and Pay, but you would never find a no-name brand item in her pantry.

Paradoxes

There were so many paradoxes – she was so prim and proper in some ways. She would only wear a dress to some functions, as that was what was expected. She always had her hair done for certain functions. We always went to church for Christmas and Easter. She played the piano for the local Sunday School. She never brought men home or perhaps we never saw her with them at our home. Yet she could be so wild, especially at parties, and her language could be very brutal. I would love to have met my grandfather and his family – that wild streak must have come from there – it certainly never came from my grandmother. I remember some of the Guscott family on my granny Thirza's side and they loved motorbikes and adrenaline and had the guts to run hotels in Butterworth, so maybe there was an adventurous spirit on both sides.

Religion

People used to often say that they could not understand where my mother got her strength from – they never realised quite how religious she was, though she found the reborn churches too over the top. This is where her prim and proper side would come out rather than her wild, flamboyant side. She felt most spiritual when she was on the beach. So many of her friends are very religious and I think they recognised the source of her strength and could see through all the bravado. One of her other favourite sayings was, "Birds of a feather flock together." She had so many of the qualities of a Good Samaritan – she always carried supplies in her car in case she had to stop at an accident. If she saw one, she would slow down and check if there was help needed. She loved to help people in need, but she would be very clear about where the money was going or who was going to spend it. She insisted that we all go to Sunday School and we all did. My gran gave us each a Bible when we were old enough to read. Thirza used to read her Bible and daily messages every day. I taught Sunday School. Most of this happened at the Humewood Methodist Church.

8.

Her friends

My mother had fantastic friends. I wanted to capture more of the essence of this larger-than-life character. My friends adored my mother and often talk of her. They found her unforgettable and they admired her. After much effort and jumping through many hoops, I got access to my mother's address book a short time before departing back to Australia, after our fifth visit to PE in 7 years. I feverishly copied out as many addresses as I could and then was badgered to return it. I wrote to as many friends as I could. I think the number of responses I received is an indication of how loved she was. She would be so touched.

She once said to me, – "friends last longer than husbands." In her case, this was certainly true. I wrote my sections of the book prior to requesting the tributes from people. It has been interesting to read other versions of my perceptions and memories.

8.1 Tributes

These are tributes from her friends and family in their own words, with minor editing where appropriate. They are in no particular order.

8.1.1 Beth Forbes

(by email from South Africa)

As a child, I remember Aunty Is as a real fun-loving person, always laughing and being the life and soul of many a party, happily tonking away on the piano while she got everyone to join her in her sing-a-longs.

I remember a tender moment when she took me by the hand down the passage in the Killarney Rd house to visit Jonathan lying in bed, days before he passed away.

And then her temper to match her fiery red hair — Aunty Is was taking Jenny, Angela, my brother Robbie and myself to school one morning — we were really late and she was hurtling round Park Drive in her little Mini when we crashed into the back of a car turning into Park Lane. She was furious with the innocent driver and then proceeded to stop cars with Grey boys or Collegiate girls in and ordered the drivers to take us to school!

After I married and moved back to Amsterdam Hoek, Is spent a lot of time out at the river with us — staying with my mom, who lives next door to me. Is enjoyed the peacefulness and tranquility of the river.

Is was great with children! On one occasion, Nigel and I had to attend a conference in Durban, after which we were flying off to Greece. Mom and Is drove up with us to Durban with our son Richard, who was then only 10 months old. When we went on to Greece, Mom drove Is and Richard back to PE from Durban. Apparently Is took her job as "child minder" really seriously and refused to sit in the front of the car, but sat at the back with Richard the whole 10 hour journey home.

8.1.2 Gaynor McGillivray

(by email from South Africa)

She certainly was a character in her hey day — not easy for her children to live with, a-larger-than-life individual who had a lot of compassion for her fellow man, was an excellent nurse, and certainly, once you had met her, you would never forget her.

On one occasion the band wasn't playing what Is wanted them to play, so she tipped the ice bucket over the leaders head!

Another time, she was travelling home in her car, and she knew she had had too much to drink and was stopped by a traffic cop. She opened her window just a wee bit, and when he requested her to get out of the car, she refused, saying "I don't know you — for all I know you are not a cop at all, just dressed like one." With that she put foot and drove to the Elizabeth Hotel, where she disappeared inside. She didn't want him to know where she lived.

She loved coming out to the Hoek. She often slept over and didn't mind roughing it on a sofa. She was instrumental in my buying No 24 Cathcart Gardens, which eventually turned into a nice profit for me.

I often used her for medical advice. She really knew her stuff.

When she and I went to the Health Farm near Pretoria (you came and had lunch with us one day), she warned me that although we were together, we didn't have to be together all the time — she would go her way and I would go mine. This was straight talking and cleared the air about our roles, which I appreciated. I went on all the morning and evening walks, played bridge etc. while she did her thing. After our two weeks at the farm, we went on to my Aunt and Uncle's farm near Hectorspruit in the Eastern Transvaal. My very Afrikaans uncle thought Is great.

She loved entertaining and made the most of her small lounge at Cathcart Gardens.

I remember her being a proud mother of her four children — all of whom I had in my play school. I know that during that time she took on night duty so that she could be with you during the day and still earn the necessary cash we all needed in those days. She and your dad went through a traumatic time when Jonathan became so ill. I think this was a big cause of their divorce, as "Schilders Disease" (I think that was the name then) was very rare and the doctors were unable to pin-point Jonathan's problem. She had to fly to Jo'burg with him where a doctor there diagnosed him correctly. He was in hospital in PE for a while, and then she took him home, as she said she could nurse him better than anyone else. Then, when Andrew became ill, and he was much younger — she came to visit me one afternoon. By then I had given up my play school and Andrew was at a nursery school in Russell Road. We were sitting in my garden room and Andrew went out to play in the garden and when I saw him feeling along the wall to find the step a cold shiver went through me, as I realised the implications. Is just looked at me and said, "I've no need to go to a doctor this time for a diagnosis." It must have been extremely hard for her (and for you) having two sons die, and then a divorce.

8.1.3 Erica Venter

(by email from the USA)

One day I remember clearly, we all went down to Settler's Park for a picnic. My mom was still alive, so we are probably looking at 1971/early 1972. We walked through the valley, where the trickle of Baaken's River flowed through. There was a sign about Bilharzias; we all learnt about that that day. Your mom crossed part of the river over some stepping stones and lost her balance as the rocks were slippery. She wailed, trying to regain her balance, which she did, but after that she laughed and laughed and laughed. Her laughter was infectious, as we all were laughing at the antic we had just witnessed.

Then one Christmas, all our gifts were ready and waiting for the early morning rip open time. Auntie Is had dropped ours off and Kurt and I were feeling the packages and trying to work out what was inside! The labels were affixed. Next morning, when we were allowed to open them, I received a panty drier, one of those round coat hanger like things with pegs hanging off them. Mom received a walkie talkie!! The labels had been put on the wrong parcels and after a phone call or working it out, we then enjoyed our gifts.

There was one Easter that I could not sleep the night before, waiting for all the Easter Eggs and chocs that we would get. We went down to your house at 5 Ferndale Road, Humewood! You had a bit of a vine creeper growing at the end of the house and we got all our goodies. There was a package of choc that was made in the shape of a cigar, vermicelli on the tobacco, they were "cigarettes": white sticks with pink ends, and other delectable stuff. We ate and ate and ate!

I remember many sleep-overs at your house. In fact I remember being taken by a cousin of yours, for my first bicycle ride and I got my foot caught in the spokes of the wheel! "Lombard"?

I do know that after my mom passed away, your mom was very very good to my granny. We remained in our little maisonette in Central, but your mom visited us often. I remember your mom in a nurse's uniform on a few occasions.

And of course, there were sad times, dear little Johnny and Andrew. How your mom continued to be after that, wow, I do not know. How you all as a family got through it all, you were all very strong.

Getting back to the good old days, I remember clearly, going to Sundays River. One of your relatives lived there — no had a holiday home there. There were huge sand dunes and we sand boarded down them for hours. Typically PE weather — the sand was always blowing about, but that is such a clear memory. Johnny was very ill, at that stage; he had had some surgery and the outing was rather uplifting for all.

I remember learning about the meandering Sunday's river in Geography, and when I was able to see what meandering was, that put it all in place.

8.1.4 Marion Campbell

(by email from South Africa)

I met Is over 40 years ago with our friends, Prinea and Jenny Smith, on Kings beach. We would gather with our children, it was a wonderful playground.

As the children grew up and went to different schools, we still kept our friendship and saw each other through both happy and sad times.

Is knew how to work hard and play hard, and I admired her when she made a decision to further her career. First she had to pass her matric which was quite something when in your 40s. Then she enrolled at the University of Port Elizabeth (UPE) for [not sure of name of degree] to do with nursing administration.

Is was always very entertaining and told us of her trip to Russia and how she got lost twice. The one time she joined the group from the boat on a bus to see a palace, but when she saw all the steps, decided to wait on a bench outside. Well, she felt it was taking a long time and was afraid they may have come out another entrance so decided to make her way back to the bus, but missed the street and kept walking until she knew she was lost and in a panic. She stopped a very old truck and tried to tell the man and woman she was off the boat. Unable to understand each other, the man told her to get in the truck, but it was very high so the man had to assist her by putting his shoulder under her rear end and hoist her in. I don't recall how she got back to the boat. Of course, everyone wanted to know what happened as she was gone when they came looking for her.

Then on another day much the same happened. They were on a bus trip to St Petersburg and again too much walking and climbing. She sat to wait for the group to return, but Is always impatient and afraid they had missed her, decided to walk and lost her way. She saw a car parked at a house and asked the man how to get back to the palace. As they could not understand each other he took her in his very, very old car to the flea market, where tourists go.

She only then remembered that she was in St Petersburg and had to get back to Moscow. She then had to ask this chap to take her to Moscow, which he did for $200. Isabel would never have done this in SA. She tells us she was so embarrassed, she sneaked on board, changed and went to the bar as if nothing had happened.

One other memory I have was my birthday when a few friends came to dinner. My mother of 90 years was present, so there was no alcohol. Is after a couple of drinks at home arrived, dressed all in black, including a cape and her wild red hair. She loved to make an entrance and shock people, and took over the evening. My mother was fascinated and fortunately could not hear some of the language. She loved Is because she was so lively and full of character.

Her health took a big change around 2003. She was unable to drive her car so depended on Angela and friends for shopping etc. As I was now retired and living in the same street, I saw her often. When the weather was good we would drive to Hobie beach and have a walk. She loved to sit on the bench and look at the sea. She would say, this is my church, then go back in memory when our children were little and she played the piano at the Humewood Methodist Sunday school.

Now that Is has moved into frail care I try to see her as often as I can.

8.1.5 Prinea Mc Gillivray

(by email from South Africa)

We loved your Mum — she was a very special and amazing woman. A character and someone one could never forget.

She was one of the first people I met after we returned from South West Africa, as it was then, to live in Port Elizabeth. We lived in a little cottage, converted into one from two old garages. It was next door to Oslo Flats, do you remember them? near S bend. We had Kathy and Donald, she had you and Jonathan. I hadn't yet met her and I was lonely. I had John's family, who were wonderful but were busy and working, so I got a job doing market research and with my precious two kids walked the beach, chatting up any poor unsuspecting female who was also enjoying the beach with their kids. Of course, your Mum was there and I went up to her to interview her. Immediately we clicked and I knew I would like to be her friend. She was, forgive me, enormous, and I thought about to have a baby, and of course I asked her when her baby was due. Of course that clinched the deal. She roared, laughed and threw sand all over my papers and told me her baby was six weeks old and at home asleep. I then proceeded to tell her all about Gay's wonderful nursery school. She listened to me rambling on, laughed again and told me she knew all about it, that somehow she was related to Gay and that you would be attending Gay's Nursery School the next term. She came home with me for lunch and that was the beginning of a wonderful friendship. You children all got on wonderfully well and we spent every sunny day with you all and with umpteen other mums and their children, Marion C and her two being some of them, on the beach.

John and I were welcomed into an amazing circle of friends and relations. The parties were always great fun, your mother being the light and soul of them all. She was so quick witted and bright, nothing escaped her sharp brain and nothing inhibited her. If there was a piano and things needed livening up, your mum would do just that, by playing, often thumping the keys and getting everyone to dance and "Get going". If there was no piano, she would tell some spicy bit of news, or a slightly below the belt joke. Once at a party at Ron and Margaret's that she felt needed to get going, there was good dance music on the gram and she said, "Come on who wants to dance" No reply, so undaunted, she picks up my dear John, all but throws him over her shoulder and starts waltzing with him. Of course everyone joined her on the dance floor. Her one desire, that John fulfilled, was to go sailing on the Hobie Cat. Quite a feat, the waves were big and they were both soaked. Next time, says your mum, I want to go out and for someone to make love to me out on the bay! John didn't oblige but she was forever asking an old friend, do you remember him? Hannah, who also sailed a Hobie. She was a remarkable woman and one I am very proud to be able to call my friend.

8.1.6 Donna Lahana

(by email from Canada)

She gave me piano lessons and I've always wanted to play like she does ... She started me on some very basic tunes, and I remember her especially when she would talk about octaves and the differences between the black and the white key tones. There would always be a "chop-sticks" thrown in just so that I could play with her. Every time she would come over to our home as kids, she would ... no, no, no, I would ... whip off the piece of felt that protected the keys on our piano in our entrance hall way at 13 Bradley Road, and beg her to play — she lifted up the entire house with music and such jovial tunes. Accompanying her tune would no doubt be her comical smile and characteristic voice. Her voice, she told me once a long time ago, would resound through the passages at Provincial Hospital, and call all her nurses to abrupt order. Being the Matron in Charge at the hospital, many knew her for her stern discipline in nursing, and I would say, her humorous side as well. She was known for her neatly kept seams, whether on the patients' beds or on her nurses' starched caps or uniforms. She would tell me countless stories to encourage me — me being a budding young nurse — which often ended up in her laughing about them so hard that you could barely understand WHAT she was saying. One of her favourite accounts, was when she adopted the name `` the witch`` because of her laugh, from her nursing staff. This got her rolling on the floor ... AGAIN! Almost hissing with laughter, she was in hysterics ...

Although there were many times we both laughed at what wild and whacky stuff went on in her stories, I always saw up a truly sensitive, tender genuineness in her heart. A love so deep for her family and friends, and a joy that sometimes was enough to keep everyone's spirits up. Aunty Is is an awesome lady and always will be ... I love her incredibly.

I hope that this is ok; it almost got me sitting in her lounge with her — it felt like yesterday.

8.1.7 Margaret Horn

(by email from South Africa)

There are many stories about Is. She was such a vibrant and sometimes eccentric character that sometimes the things she did were a little? ... Of course, one always remembers the ones that made you laugh and gasp. Garlicks which was a very high class store in PE, got a view of legs and petticoat as Isabella waited for the lift from the exclusive ladies department. She was wearing a two-way stretch corset, designed to give one a neat and trim figure and disguise the bulges. So as to look slim, Isabella was wearing one of these garments. But not for long. The torturous item had had its innings and had to come off — there and then, in front of the lift. With relief, she wriggled out of it, picked it up and put it in her bag and enjoyed the rest of the shopping morning.

When we built the big house at Marron Hill, Lovemore Park, we had a house warming party. As the rooms were not furnished, we danced in the empty lounge and family room. Isabella asked John McGillivray for a dance and he was not particularly willing, so she picked him up and carried him onto the floor and said — You WILL dance with me. Poor old John, always a slight and skinny man, didn't have a chance to refuse.

The United Party was having a very posh dinner to raise fund for the election. George and Is went along to support the cause, but alas landed up at a table directly in front of the kitchen swinging doors. The waiters for this huge affair were untrained university students and therefore did not have the aplomb at serving, which would have saved the day. So each time the kitchen swing doors opened, not only did they get a whiff of the cooking, but sometimes an extra titbit that slipped off the balancing plates. When soup was spilt over

Is, she had had enough. So picking up the bread rolls from the table, she threw them into the air and in a loud voice said, " Let's all get into the act" as the rolls spun and somersaulted in the air.

George was highly humiliated and so it was not an especially happy evening and the toffee-nosed diners looked askance at the performance.

When Is had a few drinks, she got a little wild and naughty. At a party at Gay's house in Humewood when we were all young, she wore a pretty gold lame top and a black skirt, looking very nice and elegant. But the loud music and with a dinkier or two combined, she would pull up the skirt and roll up the top and do an imitation of the belly dance. Raucously funny. Is was a brilliant nurse, firm but compassionate. She took no nonsense from the patients, but cared for them gently. She was the right person in the right job.

She was the one person in the family who could make a piano talk. Thumping away, she got the vibes jitter-bugging in a room. She loved people and parties.

When we first moved to Lovemore park, I had a tea party for friends and neighbours, introducing ourselves. I made a special spread of eats to tempt the palate. Is was always on a diet, never with great success, as she would starve for a couple of days then go on a binge. It was one of the starving periods when she came to tea. Picking up one of the scones, she lifted her hand high in the air and dropped the scone onto a plate. "Are the scones fresh, she enquired?" As they were still warm, straight from the oven, they couldn't have been fresher. But what she was actually saying was that if they were not too nice, she could maybe resist the temptation to have one, two or three. I can say that she thoroughly eventually enjoyed the tea, and said "Okay. Tomorrow I will diet!"

I have a lovely photo of Is as a bridesmaid when she was about 18. It might have been for Roy's wedding. She was a very beautiful girl. As my albums are all in storage in boxes somewhere, I can't lay my hands on it now.

A lot of Is' quirks in personality stemmed from the fact that Auntie Thirza showed a great preference for Roy and found fault with Is. In fact, I can remember going to your birthday party when you stayed in Windermere road, Humewood. Knowing that Auntie Thirza was going to be there, I dressed with great care, knowing that she had eyes at the back of her head and would pick out anything that was not quite correct. As I arrived, all smiles, she said to me — Not "Hello Margaret", but, "do you know that you have a ladder in your stocking." Well, I must have snagged it when I got out of the car, but only someone like Auntie Thirza with her hawk eyes would have noticed and certainly, only someone like her would have mentioned it for all to hear before greeting me. So, with Is, it was a similar thing. Thirza could find anything and everything to criticize and then Is would reciprocate to antagonise her mother by making sure Thirza had something to complain about.

Is went through such trauma with Jonathan and then Andrew. She carried the burden of her son's illness with great courage and fortitude. It was such a contentious issue between George and Is that it eventually broke up their marriage and Is was left to cope with the extreme stress. I salute her for her strength of character in dealing with life at such an emotional time. So it is sad to see such a vibrant character reduced to a frail little old lady, who does not recognise family or friends. The only good thing is that she is not in pain and there is no worry in her life now. She is either in a wheelchair or in bed, and she seems to spend a lot of time sleeping, which is also a good thing.

So in writing these few memories, visual pictures of Isabella have been passing through my mind, recalling old times of shared laughter and fun. None of these memories can be put into a book, but the essence of Is can be shown through her actions.

8.1.8 *Virginia*

(by email from South Africa)

I met Is (Isabella, she often signed herself) when she joined the Cape Town City Health Dept's Child Welfare section. I think this was in the late 1950s when she was married to Dr Coetzee, only child of a medical specialist and his wife. It was not a happy marriage; seemingly the in-laws disapproved of the son's choice. Then, too, the colleague with whom Is had to work was not the easiest person. The marriage ended in divorce, unfortunately not the first unhappy relationship to be terminated because Is had previously married aged 17 (though it was later annulled.)

When offered a post by her brother at his Port Elizabeth hotel, she went thence and our friendship continued through correspondence over the years. After marrying George (was that his name ?) Allnutt a girl, boy, girl and boy — in that order — arrived in due course but tragedy struck with the fatal degenerative illness of the older boy, to be followed by the appearance of the same symptoms in the younger son and a second death in the family. It may be imagined how this affected everyone. The marriage also ended in divorce.

In due course Is bought a flat and concerned herself with her family, her job, and when no longer working, joined a bowls club, writers group and returned to her piano playing. She was subject to spells of ill health, however.

Isabel was a well-proportioned woman, very attractive, extrovert, with a good sense of humour. She could be outspoken, blunt and forthright, but in a disarming manner.

8.1.9 *Mavis Brookbanks*

(by email from South Africa)

Wally was friendly with Daphne Lombard and used to often see her on his travels down the coast visiting the branches. One day we got a call from Daphne when we were in Durban, and she told us that Issey had lost her son she had been nursing for a long while. Issey needed a break as she was exhausted, and could she come up and spend a week with us. We were delighted to have her. A good part of the time she was with us, she spent entertaining us on the piano, and I can see her now, sitting on the piano stool, hammering away at the ivories — oh how we enjoyed her music and her company! She came up several times and we popped in to see her on our way to Cape Town one year, and we always kept in contact.

8.1.10 Eva

(by email from South Africa)

My slimming Salon in Port Elizabeth erupted into laughter whenever Isabel walked in, as she always had some story or other to tell us.

"Is", as she is fondly known, was a virtual laugh a minute in most situations while we were out together visiting friends, shopping or just anywhere, but especially amongst my slimming clients.

Having left PE some 19 years ago, I have made it a rule that whenever I am in the PE area to call Is or look her up.

She has never forgotten my birthday, nor I hers.

I have known Is for more years than I can remember and have shared in her sorrows and delighted in her joys.

God bless my friend Is.

Love Eva Polikoff

8.1.11 Brenda Young

(by email from South Africa)

Jenny, I am no writer, just a retired nursing sister, but I can tell you how we met and became friends.

Is and I did night duty together in the early 70's at Walton Orthopaedic Hospital. I was pregnant with our second son and studying to pass my Orthopaedics and Isabel was studying to pass her matric. We would help each other with our studies, drink lots of coffee and chat about our families, I heard about your brothers and how traumatised she was and worried about you two girls, she wrote letters all over the world to try and get more information. She is a forthright person, who always speaks her mind, as we would say in England she calls a spade a spade.

We left in 76 to go to Somerset East, where Mike was the engineer and saw the new hospital built, but we returned to PE In 1980 when he saw the Dora Nginza hospital built, by then Isabel had moved onto Provincial but we still kept in touch, our next move in 1982 was to Rhodes and I went to Settlers Hospital, Is did drive up for a visit but refused to stay overnight. Mike and I played bowls at that time and Is took up bowls at Victoria Park, not content to play lead, she wanted to skip the team. I know she was on the committee for a while of the SA Association of Retired Persons. The last time I visited she had sold her car, not well enough to drive anymore and the last card I received told me she had had brain surgery.

Hope this is helpful for you.

Regards, Brenda & Mike.

8.1.12 Dot Clifford

(by email from South Africa)

I first met your mom when we were both teenagers at the Boksburg Benoni Hospital as student nurses. They were good, happy days with lots of fun and laughter. Many happy hours were spent at the piano in the dining room, where those of us who could play did so, with the others dancing and singing. In winter we would all meet in the students sitting room where there was a fire burning and we would sit around laughing and chatting or just sit reading.

Your mum was well liked and quite popular with the other student nurses. She was also friendly with a Joan Brown, who she called Blondie. Such a lovely person, blonde and pretty. The three of us were very good friends. I know a few years ago when Joan was out from England visiting her brother in the Cape, she flew to PE and stayed with your mum for a week. Two years ago Doreen Williams (nee Walsh) and I flew down to Cape Town and motored up to Greyton to spend a week with Joan, who was then visiting her son Mike who lives in Greyton. Joan asked your mum to join us, but she didn't feel up to the journey.

Your mom and I wrote our finals together and spent many hours in the lecture room together.

One incident stands out in my memory. Your mum was on night duty and while making coffee for her and a doctor, the doctor started to get very amorous with her. To dampen his ardour, she picked him up, put him in the kitchen sink and turned on the cold tap. Just at that moment, the night sister in charge of the hospital walked into the kitchen to witness this, and needless to say, your mum had to report to the matron the next morning. Anyway, we had a good laugh about the incident afterwards.

As you no doubt know, your mum married a Peter, who had been a boyfriend while she was training. Sadly, the marriage ended in divorce and eventually she married a Public Prosecutor (forgotten his name). That marriage ended in a divorce. Your mum told me that she felt as if she was always in the dock the way he would question her. She wasn't happy. She then went to live in PE and to be near Roy and Daphne, where she eventually met your Dad. The rest is history as you would know more about life in PE than I. Your brother's death had very big impact on your mum's life. It affected her very badly.

The only connection with the Allnutt family was through my parents. Aunty Bea and my mum were teenagers together and the friendship continued after their respective marriages and I remember the two families spending many Easters and Christmases together.

Your mom loved life and was a real free spirit. On her return from Russia a few years ago, she spent a week with Max and I and it was good being together again reminiscing on the past. It's been a long friendship, which has lasted over many decades, first meeting as teenagers and now we are both in our late 70s.

8.1.13 Jean King

(by email from South Africa)

I met Is in hospital when we had both had our first babies, Jennifer and Tammy. I was battling to breastfeed and obviously irritating Isabel, she called over to me very firmly "come here" and proceeded to show me how to go about it. We shared a brandy and coke (smuggled in by one of her friends) and became firm friends from that moment.

Is neither taught me to drive — not to reverse or parallel park nor was she too concerned what gear I was in at any time, but she did teach me to do a U-turn on Beach Road in Summerstrand — what fun we had and I did get my license!

Isabel saved Tammy from drowning when she was 10 months old — took her from my arms, held her upside down by the feet, gave her a whack on the back and a good shake — such quick reactions.

When she heard that my husband had been involved in a plane crash, she was the first at the door with the inevitable "cure all" brandy and coke. She took complete control, phoned the doctor, dealt with the press very firmly, saw to Tammy and calmed me down. She was always there when you needed her and knew exactly how to handle the situation.

Full of good and bad advice, a wonderful loyal friend. We have remained friends over 46 years in spite of our transfer from Port Elizabeth in 1962. We corresponded erratically and caught up when we visited PE or she came to Cape Town

Buck, my husband of 50 years, says one of her most endearing qualities is her ability to laugh at herself.

What do I remember most fondly about Is — her sense of humour, her high-pitched giggle, the way she put her lipstick on, her love of the beach and sun, but most of all her incredible fortitude and strength in coping with all the knocks life threw at her.

8.1.14 *Edith Ellis*

(by letter from South Africa)

Isobel had hitch-hiked in England and the continent. When she arrived back from the continent she decided to start work to earn money to go home to South Africa. So she arrived at the hospital where I was working in Kent, England. We were both employed as staff nurses. I think it was 1952 or 1953, when we became friends. Isobel got on well with everyone — doctors, nurses and sisters. She was very well liked. She encouraged me to come to South Africa.

We arrived in Durban in March or April 1954 by ship and we were met at the dock by Is' cousins, Roy and family. Mom and Dad were in Johannesburg. We both worked in Durban at Addington Hospital for a short time. Is decided to go to Johannesburg to work for City Health in Soweto so I followed. We both shared a flat in Hillbrow, the place to live in those days for young people. We got on well. Isobel was helpful and it was nice to have a friend in a new country, who belonged to the country. Is made friends easily, she had a good personality and was friendly to people and I was quiet and stupid. Is had something special so she had many friends. Is bought a Mina Moons (car?) so we spent our holidays in Durban and Cathedral Peak once. We were in Johannesburg some years then Is decided to go to Port Elizabeth as she longed for the sea. We kept in touch and I missed her.

Life has been a bit cruel to your parents and those two beautiful little boys. The whole family should have had counseling, but it wasn't thought of in those days. I often think of Jonathan as I used to visit him in hospital. He was so friendly.

8.1.15 *Carol*

(by email from the UK)

So glad to hear you are writing about your precious mother. I first met her at Provincial Hospital PE in the tea room in 1981. My grandparents lived in Orange Grove and we got chatting, as usual your mother who knew everyone knew my Gran.

Granny Orsmond gave sewing lessons and your mother was taught by her, my Dad went to KES and must also have known your uncle Roy. I could never have asked my Dad though as he died in 1975, but my Aunty Joy (now 81), my Dad's sister, clearly remembers your mother.

After meeting your mom, we stayed friends; she was a delightful person with a character not matched by anyone.

Her nickname for me was Boothie, as I was married to a Booth, however, all through my divorce and marriage to David Barkes she continued to call me Boothie, she loved to stir.

Her dislike of the hierarchy at the hospital was intense, which drove her to study and get the Nursing Degree she obtained, first, writing matric so she could be accepted at UPE. She enjoyed the fact that her promotion to Senior Sister was through her achievement rather than through favouritism. She continued to be the tyrant she was in the ward, but that was because she knew what she was doing. All junior staff were quite scared of her, but in actual fact she was kind, considerate and the experience gained from her knowledge was incredible. She was loved by all her patients and was the best nurse ever! She enjoyed having the new junior doctors on her ward — she teased them and we had lots and lots of fun. I was privileged to have spent time on the same ward as her, Mozenthal 2, where we nursed the elderly, she would always say, "God help me if I end up here". I find it so terribly sad that this is exactly what has happened, though she was fortunate in having bought and moved to Park Drive Retirement Centre before she became too sickly.

Your mom resented the fact that white Afrikaners were given privileges/promotions over the more experienced, also the fact that she had nursed in the black areas and no one could see the long-term problems of over breeding. She would dwell over and over on these two feelings of discontent, they were my feelings too and many, many others, but she had the courage to speak of them openly and freely, yes hurt others feelings but she had the courage.

She enjoyed having a braai, and one evening after too many glasses of wine she drove herself home with my son John, who incidentally adored your mom and vice versa. Well John tells the story of a traffic cop following your mom in her Nissan fast back. She refused to stop and only did so close to home, then when she opened the window an inch, she said, "how do I know you are a traffic cop, and I am close to home" then off she drove. John laughs over this incident.

Another is when she visited Russia and was delayed in a market place losing her guide. She made her own way back to the ship in a little scooter/car without doors, loose wires all over and drew a ship for the taxi driver for the lift.

She adored music, opera, TV and reading *The Herald*. On the day of Diana's death, we were still in bed this Sunday morning when our phone rang early. It was your mom, she said, "Diana's dead, put on your TV". She was a mine of information and knew a lot about everyone. We used to tease her about writing her memoirs; she would laugh and say it would be a best seller. As I said she spoke her mind, even to us. She would openly criticise us and it would hurt, but she would always see it as being honest and helpful.

Your mom enjoyed entertaining and one or two years before she gave up Cathcart Gardens, her friends would give her the birthday party, each taking a plate of eats and cleaning up afterwards. She always had plenty of birthday cards and messages and the same folk would meet yearly. We met some lovely friends of your mother's. Best of all were the presents she would receive from her brother and later on Trevor. Your Birthday cards were always proudly displayed, and she was so proud of the book you co-authored *Ubuntu*, your work achievements and also of Angela's degree.

On the religious side your mother was but wasn't a believer. I took her to church in Humewood once and wanted to hide from embarrassment. While her voice was strong and loud she was not interested in the prayer side and did not hide that fact, needless to say, that was the first and last time I took her to church.

Another of your mom's favourite places was the Bell restaurant, The Terrace and also Up the Kyber. She enjoyed eating out and her favourite meal was ox tail which I often cooked for her.

Your mom was always well dressed, even at home, so I could never have her round without having first put make-up on, if she saw me without makeup she would have a go at me. Always look your best she'd say and for goodness sake grow your hair. She loved flowing locks.

So in all your mom was proud to have been a Lombard, she loved coming to us for a drink, a braai or a chat and we loved her. She made us laugh, she made our children laugh and she made her friends laugh. What a loveable, likeable person, full of life. So Jenny this is a truly wonderful gesture on your part writing up all that people loved about her. Be proud of her for the way she was and is.

We know not what tomorrow brings us, let us each live life to the full each and every day with no regrets for past rights or wrongs.

What a woman!

8.1.16 Joan Kock

(by letter from the UK)

Is was a loyal friend. We started our nursing training together, she was a bridesmaid at my wedding and years after when I moved abroad, we always kept in contact. I remember spending many off-duty hours listening to Isobel playing the piano. Her sense of humour cheered up many a patient in the wards. She cared for them and they trusted her. She was a free spirit and loved life. A character, as you wrote, but that reflected her rejection of anything fake. She was Is, and never ever played a role, that others might find more acceptable. This was what I admired most about her – the courage especially in our world, to be her, regardless. She was never shackled by convention.

I am thankful that Is was part of my life, may she be cared for in the darkness of her twilight years.

8.1.17 Ena Brito

(by letter from South Africa)

Vernon and I met your mom many years ago when both families were on holiday. It was your dad, yourself, and I think your eldest brother. We had a couple of weeks there. Vernon and your mom got on well together, as they were both full of fun. When we came back to PE your mom invited Vernon and me to dinner at their lovely home in Westview Drive. Is made a delicious roast out of kudu leg. It really was so nice. Your mom cooked very well.

When the family was living in Humewood, we used to go to the beach often and take with us whichever child was available at the time. Your mom and I spent many lovely, hot, sunny days on the beach. Of course, we both wanted to be thinner and having children we both put on weight. We were always dieting on and off. Ha! Ha!

Your brother Andrew and my son Andrew went to the nursery school at the Technical College then afterwards to the McGillivrays (Gaynor ran the school) nursery school until your brother got ill.

Your mom was a very good nurse and she looked after Andrew very well while he was at home. She was always so glad I visited her, and one day she said that it helped her to cope. Your mom was also going through her divorce at that time.

Like me your mom liked dancing and parties. Sometimes she used to dance on the table. Remember the room under the house — that is where we had our parties. My children just loved your mom and enjoyed having her at our parties. Gwen was introduced to your mom by me.

8.1.18 Leon Maree

"No, God, man you can't sleep in my spare room. You can't have good sex in there. I've moved out of my bedroom, so at least you have a proper double bed and some extra space. Sleep in there and enjoy yourselves!"

Jenny and I had barely arrived at the home of my future mother-in-law back in 1990 and with these words were were ushered into the main bedroom. It was my first meeting with Is whom I later called "ma Is" with sincere love and affection.

It was clear from the outset that I had met another of life's special characters – someone with an energetic and infectious sense of humour – who relished in surprising or even shocking those around her with some good-natured fun or perhaps an outrageous statement or joke.

I remember some of those jokes or statements being at the expense of certain individuals or groups of people. It was not unusual for Ma Is to immediately follow up with some sort of redeeming statement like "Ag, shame but they really try hard. They just can't help it!" It was almost as if her compassionate side had to have the last say.

Unfortunately, I only got to know Ma Is later in her life, at which time she already seemed largely content to entertain us in her little flat at Cathcart Gardens. I know that she had an extraordinary love for music and was a talented pianist and I regret not having heard her perform!

Over the 17 or so years that I have been with Jenny, I have met several of her childhood friends and all of them recall vivid memories of a younger Ma Is being the absolute life and soul of many a social occasion. They all loved her.

While I never got to see Ma Is in action at a party, she has certainly provided me with many a belly laugh in the relatively short time I have known her. Even the last aerogrammes posted to Jenny and I in Australia had the native African birds on the outside festooned with hand-drawn accessories – such as corks suspended from hats – even our postman must have smiled.

Ma Is spent many years in the nursing profession and other tributes in this book speak of some of her exploits and success. However, if laughter is indeed the best medicine she certainly dispensed a lot of it!

One of our visits to PE was shortly after I had participated in a triathlon event somewhere and my upper arm was quite severely sunburned. Needless to say, Ma Is' nurturing side kicked in and I was marched off to her friends at the local chemist for some attention and medication. The chemist staff seemed delighted to see her and whenever we got to be out and about with her people seemed to be attracted and connected to her. I remember a walk down Kings Beach with her one morning, when one of the McGillivray boys emerged from the surf especially to say hello to her!

Ma Is clearly had a large circle of associates and friends – several of whom have continued contact and support through to these final stages of her life – something for which Jenny and I are extremely grateful.

I entered the stage too late to be part of the earlier parts of the Ma Is story, and have relied on Jenny and others to fill in some of the gaps for me. I have immense respect for this very special lady – for the way she came through the adversity and hardships and for improving the lives of so many of her fellow men in her professional and private capacities.

Importantly for me she produced and raised Jenny, whom I have the distinct privilege of having as my wife and best friend.

Like so many others, I will miss Ma Is.

Leon

8.1.19 Gwen Bennet

(by fax from South Africa)

I met Is in the early 80s through a mutual friend, Ena Brito. Is and I became very good friends as we had similar interests, both being trained nursing sisters. We shared many interesting nursing stories. In her early years she nursed in the black townships in Johannesburg. She nursed with Nelson Mandela's first wife. At the time I was doing midwifery in District Six, Cape Town. We both enjoyed the outdoor life and used to walk to the harbour wall and have our beers cooling in the shallow waters. She loved the sea and on many occasions she said that you only had to look at the sea to know there was a higher power in our lives.

In the early 90s we enjoyed a Cape Town trip in her new Nissan Exa — needless to say she had a passion for cars. On our way, near Mossel Bay we had a puncture. She immediately removed the pistol from her suitcase and put it in her jacket pocket. Three men stopped and approached us asking if they could assist. It all turned out okay and we were soon on our way. We spent a week at her time-share which was most enjoyable.

I can recall one of her birthday parties, which she liked to celebrate at her Cathcart Gardens abode with all her close friends and family. Roy Lombard, her only brother, and us were kept in fits of laughter most of the night. Roy mentioned one of her men friends, but could not remember his name, to which Is replied, "Roy, you seem to forget that I have had hundreds of men in my life." She elaborated a bit more on the men subject which only Issie could, producing more laughter.

She always played her piano, which she had bought at 17 and everybody sang Happy Birthday.

She was always there if you needed her. Not just nursing, but in times of trouble. She nursed me after having a breast operation. I was kept in her double bed in her room. She fetched me from hospital. I spent a week treated like a VIP.

She was a deep thinker with a lust for life and a wonderful sense of humour. In times of trouble, she had the ability to give profound advice to friends, almost like a psychologist. She would come into contact with various people and after a while could almost sum up their personality. Nine out of 10 times, she was correct. She was a very clever person, much appreciated by the medical personnel, from housemen to doctors, specialists and surgeons. Sister Allnutt was almost a household name in the hospitals and remembered by every nursing student who came into contact with her during their training. I will always remember her with a deep sense of gratitude to have known her and be thankful that she was my friend.

8.2 My memories of my mother's friends

8.2.1 Prinea, Blondie and Boothie

I don't remember ever meeting Boothie, so forgive me if you're reading this and I did. I am guessing that you met my mom at work as I think you were also a nursing friend. My mom said you were beautiful with long blond hair and lived in Lelane. She also loved Boothie's partner, David. My mother adored Boothie and she was one of what I called my mom's angels. My mom had people that she felt could do no wrong and she saw as so good and pure that she would do anything for them, like Boothie and Prinea Mc Gillivray and another nursing friend, Blondie, her friend in the UK. Blondie and my mom were friends from when my mom was a teenager and Prinea used to invite my mom every year for Christmas. My mom said that Christmas was the hardest time for her as a single mother so valued anyone who was prepared to have her share a meal at this time.

8.2.10 Joan

Again, I don't think I ever met Joan. Joan was a Saturday night friend. Mom would watch TV with her and her mom every Saturday night for several years. I think sometimes she went to their flat in Central and sometimes they came to her in Humewood. My mom so appreciated having their company, as she said that Saturday nights were the hardest nights for single people. Another nursing friend.

8.2.11 Eva 1 and 2

My mother adored my friend Eva and would give her her keys to her flat so that she could see the man that she loved at the time. Eva's family had deemed this individual undesirable, so my mom helped her to be able to see him. She loved to be part of an adventure, rebel and help someone in love.

The other Eva was the owner of the Slim Set Salon in PE and they both loved to tan in the sun. They would spend hours together sunbathing. My mother adored her and missed her so when she moved to Cape Town to be near her daughter, Urlene and son-in-law, I think his name was Stanley. The world is so tiny and I attended a wedding in Cape Town and met Eva there. She was part of the same family of some friends I had made in my MBA class in Johannesburg.

8.2.12 The man

My mom had a relationship with a wonderful man for 27 years. This relationship was not known to everyone and they used to have wonderful walks on the beach almost every morning and a drink together almost every night. She helped him with the diagnosis of a relative without ever seeing this individual. It is a beautiful love story pregnant and waiting to be born. He was her best friend for all those years. He visited her in the retirement home, too, although I am not sure if she knew that. She would have been so touched.

8.2.13 Ethelina

My mom had a maid who worked for her for many, many years and she adored her. When they phoned my mom to tell her that Ethelina had died, my mom was devastated. My mom did not like people on top of her and she needed quite a bit of space. Ethelina understood my mom and knew how to handle her. She also cleaned fantastically and my mom's standards were extremely high. She would think nothing of redoing work if it was not clean enough. My mom liked a home which was almost as clean as her standards for a hospital.

8.2.6 Gwen, Marion, Gaynor, Margaret, Beth, Trevor, Angela

These are the people that, I am aware, visit my mom now that she does not really recognize anyone anymore. Sometimes they think that she recognises them and tell me some cute stories, but mostly she greets them warmly, smiles sweetly and then drifts away to her black car and her baby. Trevor said that she sometimes spoke of his father Roy and their childhood and the tin that Thirza hid money in so that Lommy could not spend it at the races. I never heard any of that. Once my sister and I arrived to see her together and she said – "It's lovely to see you two together." But that was the only time I felt she may have recognised us. Mostly she seemed content. She was so well looked after by nurses who had known her for many years. (Thank you Matron, Lindy Bray) Ange used to visit very frequently, usually several times a week and she would say that she could tell when my mom had had visitors because she seemed happier, but if she had not, she seemed down. Thank you to all of you for helping while I was living down under.

8.2.7 Tienie

Another nursing friend of my mother's – it must have been such a bonding profession. Tienie ran an old-age home in Sunridge Park. It used to be fascinating to go there. Tienie ran it like a military operation and my mom admired her for it. Some of my mom's friends gave her so much strength. Tienie was one of these friends. She had an old husband, but he used to stay in the background and I can't remember him ever saying anything. I often think of her and I don't know where she is these days. She had some sons, but again they did not talk to us at all. My mom and her would have a few drinks together and laugh from the belly.

8.2.8 *Fasie*

Another nursing friend. My mom had several gay male nursing friends — they would go on holiday together and my mom and them would go their own ways and then meet up for meals and catch up on their various escapades. They would laugh from the belly again. I remember her going to Maurice with Fasie. They would ask my mom what she thought of each partner and of course her trademark was her brutal honesty. She was usually right about how long relationships would last and how they would end. The biggest belly laughs were the comparison of my mother's predictions and the actual occurrences. My mother had such a variety of friends. I think of him often and don't know where he is.

8.2.9 *Maureen Wright*

Another nursing friend – she was a Seventh Day Adventist who worked for the church in Orange Grove and never married. My mom had many friends that she had years and years of correspondence with, but they saw each other very seldom. That's why I say nursing seems to create such bonds; they never lost touch, even though they seldom traveled to each other's areas. What was also incredible was how much they helped my mother in her hour of need – when she and Jonathan travelled to Johannesburg alone and Jonathan was not a hundred percent. They helped my mother to get him to the right specialists so that he could be diagnosed. My mom was an incredible mimic. She was particularly good at the Irish accent. She would take Maureen off....her accent and expressions...really comical so I have such a picture of her although I don't think we ever met. Where are you now?

8.2.10 Triphena and Beauty

These were the names of our wonderful domestic helpers when we were growing up, I can't remember how they left us, but they were fantastic to us and very resilient. My mom was a strict task master and they were able to measure up to her high standards and also show compassion and caring when the difficult times arose with Jonathan and Andrew. I think both would have got excellent jobs in the nursing world after working for my mom.

8.2.11 Binky and Teddy

My mom was not one for pets. Mostly the house was so pristinely clean and she had all the pelmets and skirting boards dusted regularly for our asthma so there was no thought of animals indoors. Teddy was a keeshond who was bought for Jonathan and then ended up with my dad in the divorce. Binky was a budgie that my mom had in Cathcart Gardens when we had all left home and she was very attached to. I am not sure what happened to Binky. My mom also briefly toyed with the idea of a Persian cat and we went looking at kittens at several homes, but then I think my mom could not bear to have an animal indoors so we had Teddy, but he was kept outside the house.

8.2.12 Nora Sulston

Another one who mom wrote to for years. She also worked full-time for a church in Cape Town. I stayed with her in Sea Point. Such a wonderfully gracious lady with a huge bun, generously covered and would give you a huge hug as you arrived. Mom used to talk about her husband, Ted, who I don't remember meeting, but she said he was a wonderful minister. Mom knew her son Peter, who lived in Cape Town. I visited her in the old-age home when she had moved out of her flat in High Level Road, Sea Point and I knew that she was getting old when she served Leon and I mouldy cake. She died very soon after our visit. I found out by her Christmas card getting returned to me with deceased written across it. It seemed so harsh.

8.2.13 Margaret Grieves

My godmother, also a fellow nurse that obviously worked with my mom at the time of my birth. She had daughters – I don't remember their names, I think Marjory was one of them. My mother adored her. Where are you now?

8.3 Phone calls from my mom's friends

What a fabulous surprise to get a phone call in response to one of my letters.

8.3.1 Margaret (sister of Joan, a nursing friend)

Joan was a nursing friend of my mother's and her sister married and moved to Germany — what a surprise to receive a call from Germany one night. Margaret remembered how my mother had given her the key to her flat one time in South Africa, as Margaret was visiting from Germany and had no piano to play on.

A beautiful story that Margaret told me in our hour-long chat was that my mom had posted her a copy of an article out of the *Australian Financial Review* about the importance of music. I had no idea that my mom had loved this article so much and copied it for all her friends. I posted it to her from Sydney and never heard about it again.

Conclusion

The question has been asked so often: why Is, why do this to such a hard-working, honest Christian women? It has taken me many years to think this through. I believe that my mother had so many sick people in her life because it was God's way of bringing out her beauty and talent. She was never more beautiful or gifted than when nursing. It was like a light radiated from her and she was given special powers and could handle anything. The uniform or a medical situation had the ability to switch her on. It was a calling.

My picture of her is in her pristinely starched white uniform, always immaculate with burgundy epilates and plenty of badges, perfect stockings and freshly polished shoes. She was one hundred percent punctual, reliable and professional. I don't think in all her working life she was ever late. She was cherished and loved by many and truly unforgettable.

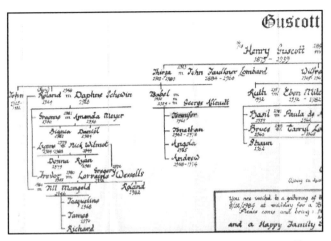

*Part of the family tree on the invitation to the Guscott Clan
Gathering received from Margaret Horn - 1984*

*Henry and Minnie Guscott
(nee Wright) with Thirza Lombard (nee Guscott) – mother
and grandparents of Is*

*Thirza Lombard – Is's mother
– 12 March 1954*

A young, pretty Is

Nursing Sister Is
at Babcock Engineering
- 1990

Is 70 years old at her beloved piano
– 13 September 2000

*Descendants of the Guscott family
with seated Is on the far left and
Margaret Horn on the far right
- December 1984*

Trevor, Roy, Lynne, Daphne and Graeme Lombard
(left to right)

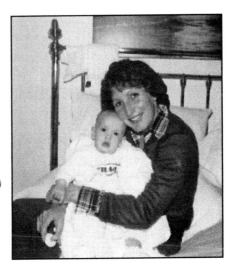

Lynne Wilmot (nee Lombard)
with daughter Donna

Tributes to 'efficient' PE hotelier

Herald Reporter

PROMINENT Port Elizabeth hotelier Roy Lombard, who died on Sunday, was hailed as a "stickler for efficiency and perfection, and a very lovable personality" by former Port Elizabeth Publicity Association director Cynthia van der Mescht yesterday.

Mrs Van der Mescht, who served with Mr Lombard on the publicity association committee, said the association had held him in "high regard".

"What he did, he did exceptionally well and he expected that from everyone else too. He set very high standards for his staff and for the tourism industry," Mrs Van der Mescht said.

She said she had known Mr Lombard and his family from the time they came to Port Elizabeth and bought the Beach Hotel while she was publicity director.

ROY LOMBARD
. . . lovable personality

partner in Bliss Holiday Apartments.

After serving in North Africa and Italy with the Imperial Horse Regiment in the Second World War he bought his first business on the Reef — a service station.

He also developed a passion for sailing and represented South Africa.

Extract from a report on Roy Lombard's death – 1993

Jenny, Is and Dave – February 1982

*Is with Jenny and Leon Maree in Port Elizabeth
circa 2000*

Jennifer and Jonathan Allnutt outside 11 Ferndale Road
– their first day at Sunday School
at Humewood Methodist Church - 1965

Jonathan Allnutt at 5 Ferndale
Road, Port Elizabeth

*Angela, with Jenny in the background,
at Cathcart Gardens November 1973*

*Ange graduating
with one of her law degrees*

Andrew Allnutt
outside 5 Ferndale Road,
Port Elizabeth – 1972

Is with Andrew
on her beloved beach
– 31 May 1973

Andrew left for Johannesburg
in June 1973

Ena Brito – December 1974

Dear Friends and Colleagues,

After 30 years of dedicated service, we are deeply saddened to share that Dr. Hugo Moser, Director of Neurogenetics research and former President of the Kennedy Krieger Institute, passed away this weekend.

Dr. Moser was originally recruited from Harvard Medical School in 1976 to become President of Kennedy Krieger and served in that capacity for over a decade. He later went on to focus his research at Kennedy Krieger on the genetic disorder adrenoleukodystrophy (ALD). For over two decades, Dr. Moser's research and study of ALD led to critical advancements in treatment. Most recently, his landmark study of the preventative effects of Lorenzo's Oil, proved the oil prevents the onset of disease symptoms for the vast majority of children suffering from this debilitating disorder.

Dr. Moser's passing is a profound loss for the field of neurogenetics, the international adrenoleukodystrophy community, and all who had the privilege of working with this great man. As anyone who knew him could attest, he was far more than a dedicated faculty member at Kennedy Krieger; he was a friend and mentor to us all.

A memorial service is planned for February 3rd in Wakefield, MA. The Institute is currently making separate plans for an appropriate memorial tribute to Dr. Moser and will be sharing more details about these plans shortly.

Cards and letters can be sent to Mrs. Ann Moser c/o Kennedy Krieger Institute, 707 N Broadway, Suite 500, Baltimore, MD 21205.

Dr Hugo Moser (1924 – 2007)
A great support to Is during and after Jonathan and Andrew's ALD, the
disease which killed Andrew and Jonathon and stamped Is as a carrier